Living

with an ...

EMO
KID

Charlie Mills

Living

with an ...

EMO
KID

Charlie Mills

NEW HOLLAND

To my eternally patient parents

This edition first published in 2008 by New Holland Publishers (UK) Ltd
London • Cape Town • Sydney • Auckland
www.newhollandpublishers.com
10 9 8 7 6 5 4 3 2 1

Garfield House, 86–88 Edgware Road, London, W2 2EA, United Kingdom
80 McKenzie Street, Cape Town, 8001, South Africa
Unit 1, 66 Gibbes Street, Chatswood, NSW 2067, Australia
218 Lake Road, Northcote, Auckland, New Zealand

ISBN 978 1 84773 273 6

Senior Editor: Kate Parker
Editorial Direction: Rosemary Wilkinson
Illustrations: Tom Hughes
Cover design: Zoe Mellors and Tom Hughes
Design: Zoe Mellors
Production: Melanie Dowland

Photographs (t=top, c=centre, b=bottom): p30 © FoxSearch/Everett/Rex
Features; p32 © New Line/Everett/Rex Features; pp34, 52(t), 53(t) © ITV/Rex
Features; p35 © NBCUPHOTOBANK/Rex Features; p52(b) © Rex Features;
p53(c,b) © David Fisher/Rex Features; p79(t) © iStock/Gary Martin;
p79(b) © iStock/Korshan Hasim Isik; p80(t) © iStock/Warwick Lister-Kaye;
p80(b) © iStock/Milos Luzanin; p81(t) © iStock/Michael Chen

Reproduction by Pica Digital PTE Ltd, Singapore
Printed and bound in Malaysia by Times Offset (M) Sdn Bhd

CONTENTS

WHAT IS EMO?

And what has
it done to
my teenager?

'Emo' is short for **'emotional hardcore'.**
Of course it is. But what's that got to do with you?
Well, first you need to know that Emo is a music
genre specialising in aggressively loud rock with
amped-up angsty lyrics. 'Emotionally-charged', if
you will. Now, imagine you are a little sunbeam of
a teenager, pootling through life and skipping
through piles of autumn leaves, then – SHABOOM
– you hear this music.

Something twists deep in your soul.
It is a clarion call, demanding you become ...

Emo Kid.

If you are living with an Emo Kid, the most important thing you need to know is that Emo Kids are a social tribe whose members are finely in tune with their feelings. Trouble is, so many of these emotions are different shades of the 'living hell' variety, which means Emo Kids tend to smile even less than Victoria Beckham in a morgue. Sure, there are good times too, but the true Emo Kid prefers to slouch about under a near-permanent cloud of woe-is-me.

Obviously, gloom is a pretty stylish business. All that black, scowling and pouting is straight from the pages of *Vogue*. Also, Emo Kids are attuned to depths of misery which ordinary mortals cannot begin to fathom. Yes, everyone has good cause to moan sometimes, but truly, life is tougher for floppy-haired teenagers. Without adult concerns like paying the mortgage and wondering if your nagging spouse is desperately itching to divorce you, there's nothing to focus on but your own personal misadventures. For Emo Kid, there is beauty in these dark emotions. Is hate not just baby-steps from love? Don't you get some of your most creative, bizarre and wonderfully mad ideas when on the precipice of a doomed love affair? Isn't self-loathing a wonderful motivator? Don't you wish you could quit making sensible lists of household chores and abandon yourself to thinking about memememememeeee?

Each Emo Kid is a veritable vortex of feelings, which can prove a challenge for the most functional of families – even The Waltons would struggle to cope with an Emo Kid in their midst. Living with Emo Kid can prove the emotional equivalent of living with a black hole: froth and frivolity get sucked in and spat out quicker than you can say, 'Cheer up love, it might never happen,' because it is happening. Right this minute.

Fortunately, this book is here to help. Learning the deeper meaning of Emo Kid's moany music, circulation-constricting jeans and curious moods will score you brownie points beyond your wildest dreams. Emo Kid is a lot of fun when you know exactly what you're dealing with.

So start cherishing those anguished, 'Nobody understands me!' wails you hear from behind Emo Kid's slammed-shut bedroom door, because by the time you reach the end of this book, you're going to be completely emotionally in tune with Emo Kid.

You might even turn a little bit emo yourself.

HOW TO SPOT AN
Emo Kid

The number one rule of being emo is not talking about emo, so if your Emo Kid won't tell you that's what he or she is, how are you supposed to know if you're living with one?

		YES	NO
1	Do they respond badly to helpful suggestions, like running a comb through the hair?	☐	☐
2	On any given day, are they wearing more than five items of black clothing?	☐	☐
3	If you downloaded a Celine Dion album for them, thinking 'Hey, this is "emotional" music: it's all about broken hearts,' might they resort to violence?	☐	☐
4	Do you suspect they enjoy looking so palpably downtrodden? Even a little bit?	☐	☐
5	Does their hair get larger, in inverse proportion to the smallness of their spray-on jeans?	☐	☐

6   Is it quite rare that they look at you, with both eyes, at one time? And without all that hair eclipsing the look?

7   If you walked into a room where they were doing a celebratory jig, for reasons unbeknown to you, would they stop as soon as you started clapping?

8   Do they save the harshest of their judgements for Paris Hilton?

9   When they listen to their special music, do they look saddened, bound up in their own angst, irretrievably lost, or all three at once?

10 Do you feel tempted to book them an osteopath appointment so a trained professional can drill them in the importance of standing up straight?

If you answered YES to five or more of these, you are living with an Emo Kid.

BEING EMO:
The Rules

RULE 1

Don't call yourself Emo Kid. Leave that to everyone else.

RULE 2

Dress the part. Looking like an extra from *High School Musical* just isn't you.

RULE 3

Fall in love with someone inappropriate. It's hardly a story if you just get together, like each other, get married and live happily ever after, is it?

RULE 4

Keep a diary (you've got a high chance of turning it into a bestselling book. Misery memoirs really sell. You could call it *No One Understands Me and I Want to Die*)

RULE 5

If your GP advises you to wear looser fitting jeans, ignore him. They might be to blame for your unpleasant itch, but isn't suffering for love what it's all about?

RULE 6

Turn the volume up a notch higher. If more people listened to music as good as yours, the world might be a better place. They just need to get past the headache stage first.

RULE 7

Take time every day to prepare your most unamused face in anticipation for the day you might be trapped in a lift with comedians Alan Carr, Simon Pegg and David Mitchell. Laughing is NOT emo.

RULE 8

You have a reputation for being sensitive so use it to your advantage... bursting into tears as you stand in a packed train carriage will probably score you a seat.

RULE 9

If no one understands your poetry, take it as evidence you are a very special human being.

RULE 10

Start using a follicle-stimulating shampoo now. When hair is such a significant factor in your lifestyle, you can't afford to dice with a receding hairline in later life.

EMO EVOLUTION

How did your little teenage sunbeam become the Emo Kid you live with now?

STAGE 1

Smiley, happy, skippy teenager. He walks with a bounce and laughs himself silly watching 'The Simpsons'. He at least pretends to listen to what his parents have to say, eats up his dinner and sometimes even says, 'thank you,' afterwards. School is OK, if only because it involves a lot of larking around and teachers accept it when he occasionally 'forgets' his homework. He can be relied upon to entertain the troops at a family gathering and is joyfully unaware of the potential for fun with the opposite sex.

STAGE 2

He attends a gig with some new friends from school and though he seems to have enjoyed himself, he walks differently afterwards. Slower. Droopier, perhaps – as if he's weighed down with thoughts and his mind is strolling along a street in a completely different world. He's not interested in introducing you to his new friends, regardless of how many heavy hints you drop. When he's not out with them, he increasingly spends his time shut alone in his bedroom and doesn't welcome you with open arms when you cheerily burst in. His hair has grown very long, but he resists your attempts to book an appointment to have it cut.

STAGE 3

His walk becomes a kind of lazy drag-and-stomp routine, which won't impress the judges on 'Strictly Come Dancing'. Not that he is interested in watching that sparkle-fest any more. He switches the bass setting on his stereo from 'clean' to 'dirty', and the local pharmacy cannot keep up with your demands for paracetamol. His fringe is so long it falls right into his eyes. He looks paler, possibly because he hasn't been out in daylight for a long time. You suspect he is seeing someone, but you have to contain your excitement / nosiness and not appear to pry, or you'll never extract any information on the topic whatsoever.

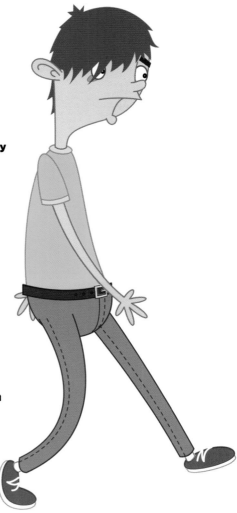

STAGE 4

When, for the 97th time, you point out his hair has become so shaggy it covers more than half his face, he hacks it up a bit with a rusty pair of garden shears and then irons the remnants straight. It doesn't improve matters. Hold on – his eyes look different. Is that eyeliner you see there? Hmmm. Whatever was going on in his love life, it's over now. But, weirdly, mourning over the lost love seems to take up more of his time than the relationship itself. Instead of chatting pleasantly over the dinner table, he reads a slim volume of what looks like poetry as you eat.

STAGE 5

For a brief moment, the grand love affair is back on. He dyes a strand of his black hair electric pink. But then the soulmate rips out his heart and feeds it to a passing murder of crows. The ensuing plummet into true emotional hardcore is dark and tortuous, but also peculiarly exhilarating. He sets his self-penned poetry to music and uploads a blog to myspace. Then, just as you are preparing a speech urging him to get some fresh air, cheer up and do something with his life, he is scouted on myspace and offered a multi-milion pound record deal.

LIVING WITH EMO KID:
DOs and DON'Ts

DOs

1   DO make sure there is at least one good mirror outside the bathroom, otherwise you are going to become uncontrollably enraged – and physically very uncomfortable – by the length of time Emo Kid takes to style his hair in the morning.

2   DO be careful what you wish for. Begging Emo Kid to listen to that special music on his iPod instead of the stereo may mean you are spared the thrashy guitars, but Emo Kid is still going to wail along out loud, which is somehow worse.

3   DO bake cupcakes. They are famous for giving even the sulkiest teenager a bit of child-like bounce. Particularly when covered with E-number-overload icing and a crusting of hundreds and thousands. We won't tell Gillian McKeith if you don't.

4   DO play your own music as loud as your eardrums can take it, just for the satisfaction of having Emo Kid burst in and shout, 'For the love of God, turn that racket down.'

5   DO throw in your own, 'You just don't understand me!' during a heated discussion with Emo Kid, because it totally wrongfoots him. Ditto, 'It's so unfair!'

6   DO put a security code on your iTunes account, otherwise your credit card is going to melt with orders for new emo music.

7   DO invite well-meaning relatives over for tea, as long as they promise to pinch Emo Kid's reluctant cheeks and say 'Oooh, look how you've grown!' in a camp *Carry On* manner.

8   DO take advantage of Emo Kid's interest in death by getting him to bury his younger sibling's hamster when it dies. It is a horrible job, after all.

9   DO download REM's 'Shiny Happy People' for your mobile ringtone and call yourself from the landline over and over again, to keep a buoyant mood in the house.

10   DO get a bouncing golden Labrador, so at least someone is pleased to see you when you come through the front door after a hard day at work.

DON'Ts

1   DON'T suggest Emo Kid dye a pink streak in his hair so he goes with the colour scheme in the living room. Being emo is all about being nonconformist, silly.

2   DON'T bother making wisecracks like, 'Where did you get that shirt, a jumble sale?' because Emo Kid probably found it in that suitcase of your old clothes in the loft, and is wearing it with a *soupçon* of irony. And a smirk, now.

3   DON'T be afraid to sneakily turn the electricity off at the mains and yell, 'Oh no, a power cut!' when you want Emo Kid to quit chatting to those mysterious online friends and go rake up some leaves in the garden.

4   DON'T offer to re-start the family tradition of reading a bedtime story, just because Emo Kid has taken up an interest in literature. You are liable to get a slap.

5   DON'T steal Emo Kid's clothes for a Halloween party. It's not very supportive, is it?

6   DON'T think, even for a second, it's safe to leave Emo Kid home alone for the weekend. He will miss you too much. Or, more likely, advertise a no-olds and no-holds-barred party on myspace. You can imagine how many hours you'll spend on hold between call

centre departments, trying to negotiate your home
insurance claim.

7 DON'T get a parrot for a pet, no matter how quiet the
house feels since Emo Kid took a vow of silence.
You will regret it when the parrot starts quoting Panic
At The Disco lyrics, throws itself off its perch and lies on
the floor, silently sobbing.

8 DON'T expect Emo Kid to take an interest in soft
furnishings, washing-up or bleaching the mould growing
in a damp corner of the bathroom. Emo Kid does not
care to sully himself with such domestic drudgery. Unless,
of course, there are threats and / or money involved.

9 DON'T enter Emo Kid's bedroom without permission.
It's for your own safety.

10 DON'T feed Emo Kid alphabetti spaghetti then expect
him to eat the mournful poem he has just created.

INSIDE EMO KID'S BEDROOM:
A Spotter's Guide

It is not often you get the opportunity to have a good look at Emo Kid's bedroom, because privacy is so closely guarded. For the rare moments you are welcomed in (or Emo Kid is out and you fancy having a good nose around) here is what you can expect to find:

25

1   Stereo **The emo hub: the music is where emo all happens. If you have any electrical engineering know-how, see if you can adjust the speakers so they do not play quite so loud.**

2   Guitar **Was it not just yesterday that Emo Kid was having recorder lessons? At least the guitar has a lower shriek-factor and more kudos.**

3   Furnishings **Notice anything, um, different here? Yes, the carpet, curtains and walls are all as black and red as raven roadkill. You are cocooned in emo-ness. The effect is a bit spooky, but also very good for getting a nice peaceful snooze. It is comforting to know Emo Kid is well-rested. Only thoughts of white, hair-shedding cats and dogs keep Emo Kid awake at night.**

4   Wardrobe **More black, mixed with shades of onyx, charcoal and tar. A pair of pink and black striped tights dangling over the top glow like a nuclear reactor at night.**

5   Poetry **Inspiring verses might be written on the wall in – surely not! – blood, while other books sit stacked up all around the room. This is evidence of great intellect. Feel free to beam with pride, but don't get all carried away and suggest you and Emo Kid start a book group or anything too happy-happy.**

6   Hair dye **It is worth stocking up on 3-for-2 deals whenever you see them because Emo Kid can never have too much of the stuff. As long as it is black. There's nothing worse than having mousey roots growing into jet-black locks. 'Mouse' is not a colour of strong emotions, thus it is not emo. Black gets straight to the point.**

7 Eyeliner and nail varnish **Despite knowing the shelf life of nail varnish is improved when stored in the fridge, do not transfer it to the kitchen without Emo Kid's permission. However, if you recognise the eyeliner as one you purchased that mysteriously went missing, feel free to snaffle it back.**

8 Box of tissues **Emo Kids have a reputation for constant weeping. Though tears may be common currency in Emo Kid's world, it is more likely he keeps tissues to deal with a harmless morning nose-blow. Do not be overly worried.**

9 Posters **Emo bands, moody-looking landscapes, perhaps the odd picture of friends. What, no photographs of you! No problem: just give Emo Kid a portrait of yourself for Christmas. Who wouldn't want one!**

10 Computer **Technically, it's for school work. That is how Emo Kid persuaded you to buy it. You will never know how much time is spent studying vs. chatting to friends online, downloading music and surfing peculiar websites. Is it too late to swap the computer for a blackboard and abacus?**

11 Unidentified mess **Be careful. Rubber gloves may not protect you. Heaven (or Hell, more likely) only knows what is in that pile. Edge away very carefully.**

12 Notebooks **Or, more, interestingly, a top-secret diary. You cannot trust yourself to look inside. No, not even to touch it. Get out, get out!**

EMO:

It's all about the music

When you understand emo music, the very core of emo-ness, your Emo Kid won't wail, 'You don't understand me!' ever again.

Fortunately, the record doctor is here to help – dotted throughout this book you'll find helpful suggestions for lyrics to quote in specific situations. Or, if you cannot find the right emo lyric to suit the occasion, just say what needs saying, mutter the name of a made-up band and use Emo Kid's favourite put-down:

'You've probably never heard of them.'

When you are trying to justify why you are not going to give Emo Kid the money for another T-shirt (which is identical to the one you can see poking out from under the sofa right now):

'As soon as you've got it
You want something else
It's not the sale that you love
It's the sell
It's not the price
That's gonna cost you
It's just the wait
That's gonna bring you down'

Dashboard Confessional: 'So Beautiful'

28

Usually Emo Kid is not feeling full of sunshine and buttercups when he arrives home after a long day at school. Serenade him with these poetic lyrics to take the edge off his mood:

'I crawl out for you
from the peaks of my joy
I crawl back into
tearing me down every time you smile
every shining time you arrive'

Sunny Day Real Estate:
'Every Shining Time You Arrive'

Had enough of living with Emo Kid! Sing this little number:

'Don't give up hope on yourself, no.
Just be patient about the fact that, be patient about
    how things are unfolding.
Because psychically, you're less ... why are you afraid
    to start?
I think you should go.
I think you should go.
You know, plan ahead, pack the things that you think
    you're gonna need,
And then just go.'

Bright Eyes: 'Clairaudients'

When you are tired but have a carload of shopping that needs unpacking:

'I'll say it out loud my voice is the only sound
So listen up, I'll spell it out
I need your help, I need it now'

Hawthorne Heights: 'I Am On Your Side'

SEVEN SHADES OF EMO

Mirror, mirror, on the wall, who is the most emo of them all?

You might have noticed that Emo Kid will do anything to avoid the poisonous words, 'You're just like me when I was your age.' To that end, Emo Kid does his best to emulate these guys, whose emo-ness is scored in emo fringes.

DWAYNE HOOVER
from 'Little Miss Sunshine'

Trapped in a dysfunctional suburban family, Dwayne escapes by taking a vow of silence for nine months in honour of his hero, Nietzsche. Dressed in a pair of black skinny jeans and a vintage band tee, he communicates only by scrawling on a notepad and chalks off days on the wall like a prisoner counting time until the end of his sentence. He seems a bit sinister at first, but be patient and you will laugh yourself senile. It goes without saying Dwayne has big black floppy emo hair, a gorgeously lopey stride, and zero interest in winning any popularity contests at school. And his family? 'No, you're not my family!' he screams at his mother, when he finally opens his mouth. 'I don't wanna be your family! I hate you fucking people! Divorce? Bankrupt? Suicide? You're fucking losers, you're losers! No please just leave me here, Mom. Please, please, please. Please... just leave me here.' Bless.

Emo rating: 7/7

MY CHEMICAL ROMANCE

Tricky: there are a lot of arguments about whether MCR are emo or not. Musically, My Chemical Romance has the heart, melody and the dark chaos. Furthermore, the lead singer, Gerard Way, has outstanding emo hair. It's either black (so classic) or dyed so platinum it's practically purple. Incredible. When he performs, Gerard gurns in the extreme, proving he runs the whole gamut of emo-tions. If that was not enough, Gerard has also publicly denied he and his band are emo. Not in the slightest. Everyone knows no true Emo Kid hires a plane to skywrite 'I AM EMO' – they just leave it to everyone else to label them. Thus, My Chemical Romance are emo. Final. Damn them for going mainstream. Turning all stadium-emo dents their angsty credibility a little.

Emo rating: 6/7

TODD CLEARY
from 'Wedding Crashers'

He could not fit in less with his family – a strict, upper-middle-class set who prize American-football-playing abilities, politics and girls in frothy dresses. Todd's emo status is born as he sits painting at an easel while the family throw a ball around on the lawn of their great estate. His father urges him to join in ('It wouldn't kill you to play some competitive sports once in a while') and Todd, hair all over his face, stripey scarf flung around his neck screams, 'Would that make you love me?' Perfect angst.

Emo rating: 5/7

STEVEN BEALE
from 'Eastenders'

When Ian's stepson returned from exile, sporting a long fringe and a wardrobe full of black T-shirts, it could only mean one thing: emo. And it goes beyond looks. Arguments with his dad? Check. Long-suffering face? Check. Ability to keep a secret that twists him up inside? Check. Complete belief that no one in Albert Square is his soulmate? Check. He has not displayed enough angst to set the emo world on fire, but for now, being emo-lite will do.

Emo rating: 4/7

EMO PHILLIPS,
US comedian

Well, he's called Emo, for a start. His hair looks pretty emo if you hold your head to one side and squint a bit. His humour is totally offbeat, which is good, but true Emo Kids are not in the business of making relentless wisecracks when they could be exploring and understanding their emotions instead of laughing at them. Plus, anyone who was born in the 50s can no longer be rightfully referred to as a 'Kid'.

Emo rating: 3/7

PETE WENTZ,
bassist, Fall Out Boy

Pete has the black floppy hair, the angsty sound and the right heartfelt / hardcore attitude. He even opened an emo-punk-themed beauty parlour – that's dedication to hairstyling. He is also a bit of a cutey, if that is your sort of thing. So far, so emo.

But going out with Ashlee Simpson dents his credibility more than confessing a clandestine Abercrombie & Fitch habit. Ashlee carries 'It Bags'. If that wasn't enough, her sister is Jessica Simpson, aka Breathing Barbie. That's a million miles from the spirit of emo, and then some. Minus points.

Emo rating: 2/7

CHARLES INGALLS
from 'Little House on the Prairie'

Michael Landon, who played Charles, was known as Emo. Why? His real name was Eugene Maurice Orowitz. Rock and roll. He wasn't known for wearing punishingly tight jeans or listening to angst-tastic, heavy-hearted rock music – in his role as Pa Ingalls, he dressed in 19th-century farmer's gear and played the violin and mouth organ. At least he's a pioneer.

Emo rating: 1/7

WHAT NOT TO SAY
to Emo Kid

Everything you know about relating to fellow human beings is wrong.

Saying 'You look nice,' to Emo Kid is tantamount to a kick in the teeth because, however contrived the look is, however many hours it takes to throw that doomed effect together, it is not meant to look 'nice'. Nice is for primary school teachers, Natasha Bedingfield and *GMTV*'s Fiona Philips. Nice is bland, boring, relentlessly mediocre. Nice is an insult.

'You'll always be Mummy's Little Angel to me.'

'How is the sunshine of my life?'

'Whaddya say we all cosy up on the sofa and watch Hairspray tonight?'

The trouble is, social etiquette is so skewed in favour of niceness so it actually takes effort not to be nice. It's dangerously easy to trip up and send Emo Kid into a whirling dervish of despair. Watch out for these humdinging wrong 'uns:

'Do you want to talk about it?'

'I DO LIKE YOUR JUMPER. WHERE CAN I GET ONE LIKE THAT?'

'Wow, nice hair. Does it take a lot of product to make it look like that?'

'HOW WAS SCHOOL TODAY, DEAR?'

'You said you wanted to go to Glastonbury, so I've bought a family ticket for all of us!'

'I know you love "CHALLENGING" music, so I've signed you up for violin lessons. Cool, huh?'

'Group hug! Group hug!'

'You're so cute when you smile'

'When was the last time we did something together as a family? I know, let's all go for a lovely walk.'

'DO YOU REMEMBER WHEN YOU WERE LITTLE AND LOVED TO TAP DANCE?'

'I was just like you when I was your age.'

'Why don't you invite your friends over for dinner this weekend? It would be great to really get to know them.'

EMO STYLE AND GROOMING

This isn't
about fashion:
it's about identity.

**Emo Kid dresses this way to be individual.
Just like every other Emo Kid.**

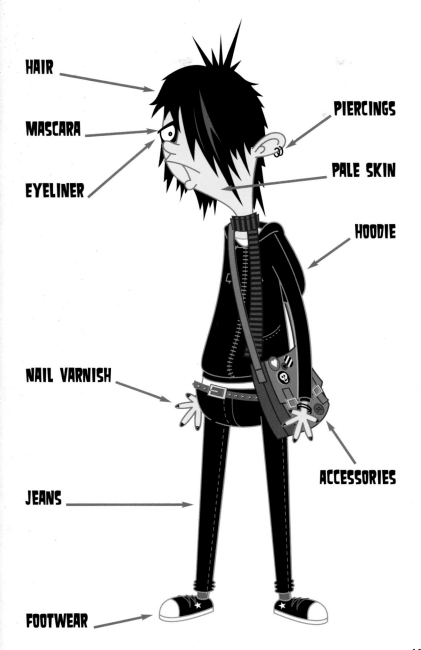

HAIR

MASCARA

EYELINER

PIERCINGS

PALE SKIN

HOODIE

NAIL VARNISH

ACCESSORIES

JEANS

FOOTWEAR

Hair It's black, obviously. Ideally it would be naturally straight, perhaps even lanky enough to suggest a deficiency of fresh fruit and vegetables. However, some Emo Kids have been known to cheat and use straighteners to achieve the look. Such hair-styling tools are also used by WAGs and 'X Factor' contestants, so it is no surprise Emo Kid hides the straighteners away. Pretend not to notice. Emo Kid will have a hard time registering the smirk on your face anyway because it's so hard to see behind that long, sweeping fringe. That hair hanging over the eyes is pretty much like a horse wearing blinkers on a busy road, but Emo Kid would rather be 90 per cent blind than deal with the world. If Emo Kid doesn't watch out for traffic and unexpected lampposts when dragging his heels down the street, a bang on the head and 100 per cent blindness is on the cards.

Jeans Why so very, very tight? In years to come historians will be more baffled by this than the mystery of how Stonehenge came to be. For now, all we know is that uncompromisingly skinny jeans are 'A Statement': Emo Kid wears them because you do not. Pipecleaner-tight jeans have few redeeming qualities, being neither particularly flattering to the figure, comfortable or possessing pockets roomy enough to house spare change. Perhaps here we have the reason: being emo is about suffering, exposing your pain and, erm, being skint.

Hoodie Tight, please, to emphasise the idea Emo Kid is a grown person trapped in a child's body. The over-small hoodie will be worn all year round, regardless of the changing of the seasons. Ideally, this garment should remain unwashed during this time, thus generating Emo Kid's signature scent. C'mon, you can't expect to be deeply synched with your feelings with the dazzling smell of Persil Automatic burning a path up your nostrils, can you? No. Impossible. The hoodie is the essence of emo.

Accessories Studded belts, leather cuffs, perhaps even a deep'n'meaningful *objet d'art* or inscribed pendant hanging from the neck by a frail leather strap – these are the essential grammar of emo style. If Emo Kid needs a bag, it's a messenger one, slung over the shoulder and across the body, and covered in badges. The rule of emo accessories is they require some reference to sensitivity (inscription: check) or suffering (studs: check). Anything else bestowed upon Emo Kid – diamond rings, Birkin bags – is liable to end up on eBay. Just so you know. However, a scarf is welcome because Emo Kid seems to live in a perpetual chill, and thermal vests tend to rob something from the Emo ensemble.

Footwear Close your eyes, and try to imagine your Emo Kid wearing tap dancing shoes or lime green Crocs. Doesn't work, does it? It completely ruins the mood. The fact is, Emo Kids spend a vast portion of the day looking down at their feet, so having a relentlessly jolly pair of shoes to gaze upon is plain distracting. That's why wearing a simple pair of Vans, black

Converse, or a stomping, chunky boot is so effective. However, anything you can buy in Nike Town is not welcome. One final note: flip-flops are not appropriate (not even black ones). The Emo walk involves copious scuffing of the toe, so the feet need protecting in order to avoid losing those precious digits. Without toes, there will be no more games of This Little Piggy Went To Market. Too cruel.

Pale skin The sun is Emo's enemy! Fake tan is Satan in bottled form! It helps if the skin isn't just a greyish pallor, but also has big dark circles under the eyes from all those late nights staying up reading tearjerking poetry or, er, headbanging. No bonus points for black eyes from said headbanging though: that's pushing the look too far.

Nail varnish Smooth black polish, as if the fingernails have been dipped in tar or the well of loneliness. Very dark red polish that gives the hands the appearance of an afternoon spent scrabbling around in dried blood is good, too. Chipped varnish and bitten nails work because they prove the wearer's sensitivity and suffering.

Eyeliner Pretty-pretty isn't the order of the day here. The black liner is not applied delicately, but as if the pencil was held in the fist of a particularly clumsy chimpanzee and then ringed around and around the eye in a deep, wild scrawl. It's a cry for help. An ancient proverb describes the eyes as 'the window to the soul' – you have been warned.

Mascara **Oh, what dilemmas abound. Should Emo Kid wear waterproof mascara upon the lashes, because on any given day crying is very likely? Or non-waterproof so the face shows really dramatic evidence of weeping? Tricky decision. It's also worth knowing that waterproof mascara is very difficult to remove (bleach-based cleaning products are not recommended for the delicate eye area) so after several weeks of continuous wear, the lashes may actually get so weighed down they fuse the eye shut. Emo Kids get a kick out of being introverted.**

Piercings **Some Emo Kids look like a magnet loose in a paper factory. Ears, noses, eyebrows, lips, tongues, unmentionables – is nothing sacred? Such behaviour cannot be encouraged, because otherwise airport scanners of the future will be on constant high alert. National security is at risk.**

8 REASONS TO RATE EMO GIRLS

Any fool knows Emo Kids come in both sexes.

We only say 'he' in this book for the sake of grammatical correctness and because 'he or she' takes too long to type. Androgyny may be the order of the day, but some Emo Girls like to push the envelope and should be applauded thus:

1 SHE MIXES MONROE WITH EMO

2 SHE EDUCATES ON GUYLINER MATTERS

3 SHE SETS THE BAR FOR MINIMAL EYE CONTACT

4 SHE HAS STEEL BELOW THE SURFACE

SHE LIKES HER BOYS BEAUTIFUL

5 SHE WILL NOT CATCH CHILL, DESPITE WEARING FEW CLOTHES

6 SHE RISES ABOVE A DENIM WAR

7 SHE MAKES ODD CLOTHES LOOK CHIC

8

1 **She mixes Monroe with Emo.** Black hair is so ubiquitous in the emo world that if you want to stand out, you need a shot of Marilyn Monroe. Platinum blonde, please, not a WAG-esque shade of yellow, or you may as well cover yourself in fake tan and wear a Juicy velour tracksuit with 'bad taste' embroidered across the bottom. So, yes, hair can be silvery, glow-in-the-dark blonde.

2 **She educates on guyliner matters.** Emo Girl has a key advantage over her redundant-nippled counterparts: better make-up. She would never make a rookie error like using a permanent marker pen to draw around her eyes, and she will advise her Emo Boy friends to procure themselves a nice, soft crayon-y kohl in order to stop looking like the Hamburgler.

3 **She sets the bar for minimal eye contact.** If Emo Kids require 2/5 of the face to be covered by hair, Emo Girl goes for 3/5. A bigger barnet to play with, you see. The less she makes eye contact, the easier it is for her to cultivate a bewitching air of mystery. Also, hiding behind that hair means she never gets inadvertently drawn into small talk about Britney Spears's early pop career and the like.

4 **She has steel below the surface.** You might not immediately think Emo Girl is self-confident. Look again. She wears whatever she wants. If that's not proof she's got sass spilling from every pore, what is!

She likes her boys beautiful. **If Emo Girls liked their boys butch, you can bet Emo Boy would be out there building a neck so muscular it resembles the elephant foot gently rotating in the window of your local kebab shop. We are all spared.**

She rises above a denim war. **Seeing as Emo Boys work skinny jeans as well as, if not better than, Kate Moss, Emo Girls need a comeback. Tutus are the answer. Three good reasons: they're outrageous, girly, and outrageously girly.**

She will not catch chill, despite wearing few clothes. **There is a rumour Emo Girls are trying to set a new world record for the amount of sweatbands, cuffs and brightly-coloured bracelets worn between their wrists and elbows. Presently, this rumour is unverified. However, the good news for all those involved in this sport is that covering the wrists can keep the body about five per cent warmer, because the pulse point is protected from draughts.**

She makes odd clothes look chic. **Young ladies who are inclined to feel chilly may also be interested to know that fingerless gloves are bang on emo trend, particularly when worn indoors. Parents who are looking for an excuse to turn down the thermostat, take note.**

GLAMOROUS EMO GIRL

EMO VENN: GLAMOUROUS EMO GIRL

Emo Girl faces a nightmare situation. Basically, she wants a platinum blonde style, cut long and straight to frame the face, but cropped very short at the back. Any on-trend hairdresser knows this is a 'Pob', the sharp blonde bob popularised by Posh Spice in autumn 2007. With such anti-emo spirits about, Emo Girl cannot risk a trip to the salon. Instead, she channels Edward Scissorhands and hacks up her hair in the privacy of her own home. Or, your home. Whichever way you see it.

WARNING!

The Emo Cash Cow

A special note on band merchandise: underground music doesn't make very much money. There is nothing a crafty-minded band won't do to squeeze another buck out of your Emo Kid.

CAN ANYONE BE EMO?
Judge for yourself

The world would be a better place if everyone were in touch with their feelings. Unfortunately, not everyone can carry off the look. For example…

Antmo & Decmo

Bushmo

Trevor McDonaldmo

Dame Judi Denchmo

Bruciemo

EMO CINEMA
Morose movies

Emo Kid loves popcorn as much as everyone else, as long as it can be eaten in the dark of the cinema and he has time to retrieve the stray corns lost in his fringe.

Here are a few of his favourite films.

Home Alone: Lost in New York	Home Alone: Lost in Oneself
The Devil Wears Prada	The Devil Wears Black
Highlander	Highmaintenance
Oceans 11	Oceans of Tears
Sweeny Todd	Stroppy Todd
Brokeback Mountain	Brokeback Moaning
Shrek	Shriek
American Pie	American Sigh
PS I Love You	PS I Hate You
The Englishman Who Went Up A Hill And Came Down A Mountain	The Englishman Who Went Up His Own Arse And Never Came Down

SCARY EMO KID

EMO VENN: SCARY EMO KID

With his best hair-growing years behind him, Hannibal Lecter cannot hide his face behind a mop of hair, so a hockey mask is brought in. He is super-intelligent, alienated by society and has a tenuous hold on sanity. Ditto Gordon Brown, except he manages to win votes, smile occasionally and look pretty respectable in a suit. Scary Emo sits somewhere inbetween. Worrying.

EMO KID
In the Wild

Witnessing Emo Kid's behaviour in your shared home can sometimes be disturbing. It makes you worry about what Emo Kid gets up to in the big wide world. No need to worry: spy away to your heart's delight right here...

In gig heaven. **Emo Kid probably has a plectrum in his pocket, just in case the bassist is taken ill and a replacement is urgently needed. The dream may one day come true, but tonight Emo Kid is lost in the music. Or just plain lost. Emo Kid is not known for being the first one in the mosh pit – instead he watches in silent contemplation, feeling a shimmering shiver exude from the crowd as his heartstrings get plucked raw. If you are ready to chauffeur Emo Kid home, it is advised you sit outside in the car and wait politely instead of poking your head inside the venue and witnessing the screaming release of emotion in graphic technicolour.**

Soaking up coffee culture. **Funnily enough, Emo Kid's strict ethical code goes AWOL when in a hundred-yard radius of a Starbucks Frappucino. The only way Emo Kid can justify boosting the profits of a high-street homogenising, corporate-cloning, soulless coffee shop is to sit there for hours with just a copy of *Descartes: Selected Philosophical Writings* for** company. In that masterstroke, Emo Kid gets his depth back. And those frappucinos are mighty tasty.

Ripping open emotional veins. **Where better to pull open the wounds of unrequited love than at an underground poetry recital? Listening to a fellow poet share their pain, ranting in angry seven-syllable verse and gently weeping through it all, pushes Emo Kid right to the verge of catharsis. But that is not wholly responsible for Emo Kid's new-found glow, no. That is down to the sweet, sweet knowledge that attending an underground poetry recital makes Emo Kid officially of a higher intellectual level.**

On the street. **OK, so Emo Kid is making a rare public appearance, but that does not mean he is anything but anti-social. What's an Emo Kid to do? The answer is obvious: shut out the world and tune into your feelings at the same time by listening to music. White iPod earplugs do the job, but wearing massive headphones scores big emo kudos, even if the pavement isn't wide enough to accommodate the armchair-sized speakers strapped to the side of Emo Kid's head. There is nothing about this look that encourages strangers or tedious neighbours to make conversation.**

Hanging out. **Deliberately vague, this. 'Hanging out' could refer to sitting around chatting in a friend's bedroom, scaring small children in parks or being eyed suspiciously by confused security guards in shopping centres. It is basically a description of doing Nothing Much Really, designed to worry parents.**

EMO:
It's all about the music

Have you ever thought, 'Sod it, I give in. Forget about me and my needs, just go out with your emo friends and have a jolly time (or a miserable one if you prefer)'! But of course, you do not want to burden Emo Kid with your woes. If you love them, set them free, hmm! This one is for you:

'Looking back on all the times we strained to have,
Vacant eyes a sometimes smile.
Thinking back on all the things we almost did,
I hope you had a good time.'

Senses Fail: 'Angel And I'

For those quiet Sunday afternoons when you get sideswiped by a gory vision of the future, suddenly realising Emo Kid could well be the person who chooses your nursing home:

'Tied up, in thoughts
Of what to do
With the body when
The engine rots'

Embrace: 'If I Never Thought About It'

If you are hoping your Emo Kid is just going through a short-lived phase, quote this little nugget to reach out and bring him back from the dark side:

'Just think of us together whenever you're down...
Are you okay...
Are you alright...
Do you count down the days like I count down the nights...
You know that I wait and I wait and I wait...'

Sense Field: 'Are You Okay?'

Ideal for when you are waiting for Emo Kid to finish doing his hair so you can go to Sainsbury's:

'But I'm getting tired all over again so hurry up
And get here because I'm still waiting...
Just like I've always been.
I'm getting tired of standing around,
Just sitting here and waiting to be found.'

Texas Is The Reason: 'Back And To The Left'

EMO KID
In Love

In a world populated by robots, Emo Kids are unashamedly romantic. An Emo Kid without an object of desire is like George Bush without something stupid to say: rudderless.

That's not to say every Emo Kid has a partner, no. In fact, emo relationships are best conducted at a distance. There is much more potential for miscommunication, misunderstanding and unfulfilled yearning – the very lifeblood of emo existence.

Emo Kids are so full of feeling they fall in love very easily. It is possible for Emo Kid to extract 'A Moment' from an exchange with a cashier in Marks & Spencer. In Emo world, it does not take much to get a grand love affair going.

One sideways look, another carefully-timed blink, perhaps even a cold shoulder. This evidence points in one direction only: love. Strike up a classic emo tune into the background and Emo Kid's heart is signed, sealed and delivered.

Emo Kid is not afraid to say 'I love you.' and at any given moment can be found musing on a new poem for his loved one. Emo Kid would never use 'I LUV U' text-speak when a 12-page handwritten love letter would do. He is only a hop, skip and a jump away from leaping up and down on Oprah's sofa.

Given Emo Kid's sensitivity, you might be surprised to know emo music is more famous for angry tunes than soppy love songs, but really the two are one and the same. Take 'I Don't Love You' by My Chemical Romance, for example. It tells the story of a girl breaking up with her boyfriend. He is destroyed and angry, which makes what he has to say profound and poetic. With rage, passion and dejection defining every syllable, he challenges the girl to say, 'I don't love you / Like I did / Yesterday' – a line that does not so much tug at the heartstrings as rip them right off.

But, as the slogan on one special emo T-shirt says, 'Prose before hos'. The message being, it is better to have an eloquent grasp of the English language than to have your true love by your side. Otherwise, you and your loved one are headed for a life of domestic bliss in a cute little cottage with roses round the door, which is the least emo thing in the world.

THE EMO
Hate Parade

It might seem Emo Kid is just plain miserable all the time, but that's not the case.

True Emo Kids are those who experience deeper emotions than other people, and aren't afraid to show them. Isn't it better to deal with your darkest emotions rather than bottle them up until eventually they spew out of your rectum? You need to know the nuances and shades of every mood to really understand Emo Kid. Use this as your introduction.

Life is not all hugs and puppies, sadly. Normal, everyday things like catching sight of Simon Cowell on the TV can really get Emo Kid down. That man not only gives black a bad name, but he is also responsible for force-feeding the nation seriously rubbish music. His work on 'X Factor' makes him the high priest of pop puppets and it is distressing to see so many people buying his records and – worse – fancying him. So arrogant! So smug! Such appalling trousers! Complete anti-emo.

Black Cloud rating: 3

While on the topic of music, TV talent competitions, and all that is wrong with the world, Girls Aloud never fail to give Emo Kid a twinge of sadness. Their Barbie-doll come-hither looks are one (objectionable) thing but their biggest crime is that their tunes are so goddamn catchy, and are constantly on the radio. The shame of being caught humming along to 'Love Machine' is worse than wetting the bed.

Black Cloud rating: 5

School is some sort of sick popularity contest. Occasionally an English or Art class might capture Emo Kid's imagination, but that cannot compensate for the idiots who drag their knuckles around the halls. Sometimes it would actually be preferable to spend one's time trapped in a hot lift full of people with unfortunate digestive problems than inside the school gates.

Black Cloud rating: 4

If school is unsafe, the outside world is not much better. First problem: rain. It is good the universe can show its emotions with a cathartic weeping session, but rain causes havoc with the hair. Even if Emo Kid whips up a hood in time, the moisture in the atmosphere can cause carefully-straightened hair to expand like a ragged sponge in a washing-up bowl.

Black Cloud rating: 5

Other cosmetic worries, **like running out of eyeliner and hair that falls out due to overuse of straighteners and abrasive dye, can cause sleepless nights that only contribute to the wretched state of affairs.**

Black Cloud rating: 4

Thankfully Emo Kid goes through emotions with astonishing speed, so these storm clouds do not take long to blow over. Be warned though: any loved-one who crosses Emo Kid during one of these abovementioned episodes can expect things to end badly. Sorry about that.

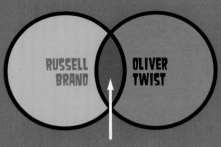

DICKENSIAN EMO KID

EMO VENN: DICKENSIAN EMO KID

Emo is rooted in the Goth tradition, but please – *please* – do not say this out loud, because Emo Kids can get quite upset when confronted with evidence another tribe ruled the world before them. Emo Kid will not be happy to be linked to *heat* favourite Russell Brand, but let us look at the similarities: big, hyper-styled black hair, tight trousers, quick witted, passion for long words. But Brand is way too upbeat. Dickensian Emo comes with a dash of, 'Please Sir, can I have some more?' rejection.

HOW TO
Embarrass Emo Kid

It is hard to tell whether Emo Kid is antagonistic or self-effacing. Embarrass them and find out their true mettle. It's worth having a rapid exit strategy planned well in advance, but you will enjoy seeing how far you can push it.

STAGE 1:

Play Westlife at top volume, and loudly ask Emo Kid to please turn the music down. How does that go down!

STAGE 2:

Turn up at school in Emo Kid's lunch break to deliver a hug. Don't let go. Nice?

STAGE 3:

In secret, buy tickets for the My Chemical Romance tour and turn up wearing your best beige slacks. When you see Emo Kid, say, 'Hey dude, fancy seeing you here!' Success?

STAGE 4:

Sign Emo Kid up for a part in the local pantomime. Drama is a great way to express those emotions, after all. Is playing Cinderella the highlight of Emo Kid's life so far?

STAGE 5:

Pack Emo Kid off to polo lessons so you can loudly tell everyone that he is new-best-friends with Princes William and Harry. Fnar fnar. Is he proud?

STAGE 6:

Take Emo Kid to family counselling sessions, so you can really get to know each other in a right-on manner. Do you break through?

STAGE 7:

Make a call to Trinny and Susannah and arrange a surprise makeover for Emo Kid. On primetime TV. Does he call OFCOM to complain?

STAGE 8:

Launch a Parent & Emo beauty pageant to show your support for Emo Kid's style. Is this the beginning of something beautiful?

STAGE 9:

Organise a stripper for Emo Kid's 18th birthday party. Has he filed for divorce yet?

STAGE 10:

Wear your pants on your head. All kids love that. Don't they?

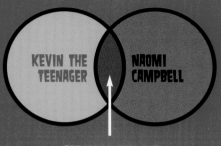

KEVIN THE TEENAGER — NAOMI CAMPBELL

STROPPY EMO KID

EMO VENN: STROPPY EMO KID

'I hate you, I wish I'd never been born,' is the favourite line of Harry Enfield's Kevin the Teenager character, closely followed by, 'It's so unfair.' Perfectly emo, if only his shaggy hair wasn't so orange and his shirts so lime-green-loud. Supermodel Naomi Campbell may have a temper you would not like to be shut in a soundproofed room with, but at least she can dress well, as shown when she turned up for community service wearing couture clothing. Stroppy Emo Kid sits bang between the two.

HAPPY BIRTHDAY,
Emo Kid!

While birthdays are traditionally a celebration of another year of life, Emo Kid has a new spin: for every birthday, you're closer to death.

For those who love nothing better than planning a good ol' knees-up, you are advised not to stand outside the school gate with a bunch of balloons handing out invitations to Emo Kid's birthday. Not every classmate is a friend. Hijacking Emo Kid's myspace and inviting his 1,371 online 'friends' to come out and play is not a good idea either.

There is a chance Emo Kid may not want you involved in the birthday party at all. Unless you would like to purchase a crate of tooth-tingly sweet alcopops, in which case you may be permitted to wait outside in the car while Emo Kids' friends do emo things in your house. Your neighbours may wonder what is going on as you forlornly spy through your own living room window, but c'est la vie.

However, being miserable is not your department – you are not the Emo Kid in this house. Stick to what you are best at: planning a nice family party. Get everyone together, even if you have not sustained a conversation of more than five minutes in the last six months.

You'll need to bake a cake for the occasion. Emo the cake up a bit by icing it black and piping a few chilling lines of poetry on the top. Better still, make it a few months before the big day, so the cake is as cobwebbed and mouldy as Miss Haversham's wedding cake. She is the Emo Mother – you have to admire her decades-long commitment to doing nothing but sitting around and weeping through her heartbreak.

NOTE: PLEASE TAKE EXTRA CARE WITH BIRTHDAY CAKE CANDLES.

Emo fringes are notoriously long and there is nothing like the stench of burnt hair to cast a shadow over the celebrations, never mind the trauma of having short, patchy hair like a wigless Joan Collins. Poor Emo Kid.

PRESENT WISH-LIST*:

- 'Coleen X' – the celebrated fragrance from Wayne Rooney's girl, which presumably smells of dirty football kit, stale champagne and fake tan

- A pair of tickets to see *Lord of the Dance*

- A large, bright sweatshirt with 'Abercrombie & Fitch' emblazoned upon the chest in large, shouty letters

- A handbag-sized pooch in a Louis Vuitton carry-case. Maybe a diamante lead as well, for running the little ferrety fella around the park

- A lifetime subscription to *Hello!*

*THE AUTHOR CANNOT ACCEPT RESPONSIBILITY FOR EMO KID'S SATISFACTION WITH THESE GIFTS. YOU FOOL.

It is traditional for families to take a holiday together every year. Holidays are so deeply embedded in our culture that many people view a week in the sun as a human right. Emo culture, however, sees things rather differently.
A vacation involves being separated from friends, having no privacy and being surrounded by the sort of people Emo Kid takes great pains to avoid at home.

BUT NO MATTER.
YOU ARE ALL GOING ON HOLIDAY AND THAT IS THAT.

The first hurdle is getting through customs. No, not because Emo Kid has made it onto MI5's Most Wanted list, but simply down to the fact Emo Kid no longer looks anything like his smiling passport photo. Customs officers tend to be suspicious of people who cover their whole face with hair. Suggest Emo Kid goes for a more natural look, just until he boards the plane.

Now, where should you go? Typical hot beach holidays may not be the exotic paradise for Emo Kid they are for you. Admittedly, sweating so much your eyeliner runs is pretty undignified. And because Emo Kid is so unused to bright light, a single day of sunbathing will turn his skin into something resembling beef carpacchio.

EMO PACKING ESSENTIALS:

- industrial-strength suncream

- swimming hat
  (frizzy hair must be avoided at all costs)

- Vaseline
  (in the heat, drainpipe jeans can actually become welded to the leg)

- iPod, plus the largest, most anti-social speakers the airline's baggage allowance will permit

- waterproof eyeliner

What about going away to sea? A cruise is one option: it certainly offers more breeze than the beach. Emo Kid might even make friends with the on-board entertainers – they are definitely unafraid to express themselves. Very Emo. If only cruise ship entertainers weren't so fond of using 'jazz hands' to show their emotions.

Sailing is also a possibility, though it will be hard for Emo Kid to shout, 'Leave me alone,' with any authenticity when you are all trapped on a boat roughly the size of a Volvo.

If you are secretly hoping your Emo Kid will shed his high-maintenance beauty routine, take him camping. Once Emo Kid discovers there is nowhere to plug in the straighteners, he might ease up a bit. Who knows, you might even bond over the last wet wipe. Maybe.

Center Parcs, often considered an easy option for families, offers something for everyone. While you cycle in the forest trails, splash around on the lake and get swimming costume burns on the water slides, Emo Kid will certainly enjoy pouring scorn on the whole thing and is sure to get emo points for being such a nonconformist among the fun-by-numbers drones. Like you.

Skiing is a potential in the winter. It scores points for being cold and the fact black looks really good against the snow. Hurtling downhill into an ice-laden headwind isn't going to do any favours for Emo Kid's fringe, but if you take him to the ski resort of Emo in Ontario, Canada, he might just forgive you for it.

ENCOURAGING
Positive Thinking

Co-habiting with Emo Kid does make you worry. Enough of this, 'Nobody will ever love me,' malarkey. It's time to harness the power of positive thinking and pump up Emo Kid's self-esteem. Success is all about attitude. Heck, if cosmic ordering can rescue Noel Edmonds from Crinkly Bottom, who knows what positive thinking could do for your Emo Kid.

Unfortunately, an innate emo quality is the ability to believe the worst in everything. Challenge Emo Kid to face the happy truth with the following simple exercise – the more NOs he scores, the greater the proof that good things can happen.

	YES	**NO**

This is
your bicycle...

1   Does a dog urinate against your bicycle?   ☐   ☐

Does anyone steal your bicycle?   ☐   ☐

Do you forget which railings you
chained your bicycle to and have to
walk home in the rain?   ☐   ☐

You decide
to cut your
own hair...

2   Do you end up looking like your mother?   ☐   ☐

Does your mother scold you as severely
as she did the last time you cut your
own hair, aged four?   ☐   ☐

Does the rugby-playing boy with the
sensible short back and sides vow to
get his hair done like yours?   ☐   ☐

	YES	**NO**

It's time for a shower...

3   Do you get slashed to death by a crazy transvestite, like in *Psycho*?   ❏   ❏

Do frogs pour out of the shower head?   ❏   ❏

Do you slip over and paralyse yourself from the waist down, thus making it very difficult for you to shoehorn yourself into skinny jeans?   ❏   ❏

You get a new handset for your birthday...

4   Does your phone melt with the amount of emotion pouring through it?   ❏   ❏

Does your ringtone switch itself to something by James Blunt?   ❏   ❏

Does it throw itself out of the window?   ❏   ❏

	YES	NO

This kitten
is yours...

5   Does it meow brightly and give you
    a sinister cat smile when you ask,
    'Why does everyone hate me?'   ☐   ☐

    Does it spill your boiling-hot cup of
    tea over your face, causing a scar
    that looks like a purple moustache?   ☐   ☐

    Does it leap from your arms into the
    canal, making it look as if you were
    trying to drown it deliberately?   ☐   ☐

There we have it: proof the world is a
happy, smiling place. What's to be sad about?

EMO:
It's all about the music

This will get Emo Kid's attention when he's is in a bit of a mood with you and refusing to talk. Quote to begin negotiations:

'This hole you put me in...
Wasn't deep enough.
And I'm climbing out right now.
You're running out of places.
To hide from me'

My Chemical Romance:
'It's Not a Fashion Statement, It's a Deathwish'

When you are wondering if your Emo Kid was brought up in a barn, despite never having lived on a farm:

'Haven't you people ever heard of closing a goddamn door?'

Panic At The Disco: 'I Write Sins Not Tragedies'

When Emo Kid has uttered one or more four-lettered words that would not be appropriate for having tea with the Queen:

'Watch your mouth
Oh, oh, oh
Because your speech is slurred enough
That you just might swallow your tongue
I'm sure you'd want, want to give up the ghost
With just a little more poise than that'

Panic At The Disco:
'Nails for Breakfast, Tacks for Snacks'

When Emo Kid has been taking the whole introversion thing a bit too far, and you really fancy a nice, upbeat conversation:

'Because I can't stand this silence, it
speaks too loud for me
A song that fails and fails me once again
denied release
And left
Words, words away from you
From where my heart wants to be'

Rites Of Spring: 'In Silence / Words Away'

WHAT'S GOING ON...
... inside Emo Kid's Head?

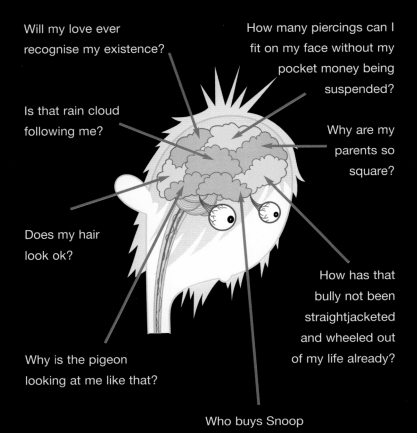

Will my love ever recognise my existence?

How many piercings can I fit on my face without my pocket money being suspended?

Is that rain cloud following me?

Why are my parents so square?

Does my hair look ok?

How has that bully not been straightjacketed and wheeled out of my life already?

Why is the pigeon looking at me like that?

Who buys Snoop Dogg records?

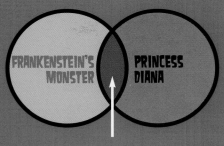

MISUNDERSTOOD EMO KID

EMO VENN: MISUNDERSTOOD EMO KID

Frankenstein's Monster is created by a man with little idea of how to cherish his nearest and dearest, and is abandoned. He is forced to spend his life on the run from the turnip-heads who persecute him and is desperate to find someone who will understand him and love him for who he is. Princess Diana had a similar story, but she had the advantages of good cheekbones and a strong fashion sense. Obvious emo middle-ground there.

COMMUNICATION
Tips

Sometimes Emo Kid can be hard to talk to. Shyness, thoughtfulness and introversion are key elements of emo.

Try this script to kick-start a conversation:

'All the better for talking to you'

Makes mournful growling sound, like a polar bear on the last remaining iceberg

'Wait a sec, I'll just grab my wellies'

'You're so understanding. I love you so much I think I might burst'

Whips off emo wig and says, 'I love you too!'

Emo Kid is possibly being sarcastic, but nevertheless this is the nicest conversation you've had with them in weeks. Quit while you're ahead.

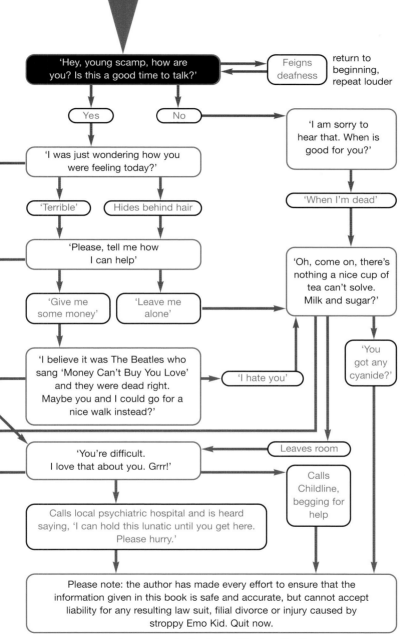

'Hey, young scamp, how are you? Is this a good time to talk?'

Feigns deafness → return to beginning, repeat louder

Yes

No

'I am sorry to hear that. When is good for you?'

'I was just wondering how you were feeling today?'

'When I'm dead'

'Terrible'

Hides behind hair

'Please, tell me how I can help'

'Oh, come on, there's nothing a nice cup of tea can't solve. Milk and sugar?'

'Give me some money'

'Leave me alone'

'I believe it was The Beatles who sang 'Money Can't Buy You Love' and they were dead right. Maybe you and I could go for a nice walk instead?'

'I hate you'

'You got any cyanide?'

'You're difficult. I love that about you. Grrr!'

Leaves room

Calls Childline, begging for help

Calls local psychiatric hospital and is heard saying, 'I can hold this lunatic until you get here. Please hurry.'

Please note: the author has made every effort to ensure that the information given in this book is safe and accurate, but cannot accept liability for any resulting law suit, filial divorce or injury caused by stroppy Emo Kid. Quit now.

THERE — DOESN'T BONDING FEEL GREAT?

THE CIRCLE OF TRUST
Emo Kid's friends

Emo Kids might seem quiet or shy, but in the right company they are wild social animals and will openly divulge deeply personal secrets. If you want to really connect with Emo Kid then you must manoeuvre yourself into a position where you join the circle of trust.

Though your own Emo Kid may sometimes seem uncommunicative or hostile to you, his friends can be more easily cracked. Typically, teenagers are are rude and foul-mouthed to their own kin, yet nothing but sweetness and light with a friend's family. Take advantage of this.

DO NOT BE AFRAID TO BUY FRIENDSHIP.

Welcome the gang into your home with chocolate and free rein on the remote control. Watch for the friend wearing trousers that enable the circulation of his legs to flow freely. He is clearly less committed to the emo cause. You want your Emo Kid to become best mates with him. Inevitably there will be one or two friends in the crowd who arouse your suspicions – perhaps they have too many piercings, look like thieves or appear plain barking mad. However, warning your Emo Kid against these characters will only push him towards them. Steer Emo Kid off this course with the help of mild flirting.

Offering invaluable domestic services like drink-pouring and late-night chauffering will score you brownie points with the group. Soon enough, they will feel comfortable in your company. When you hear a little nugget like,

'So when are you having that party?'

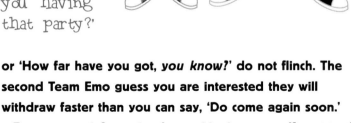

or 'How far have you got, *you know?*' do not flinch. The second Team Emo guess you are interested they will withdraw faster than you can say, 'Do come again soon.'

Extract more information by positioning yourself next to the front door 24/7 so you are always first to answer the doorbell when Emo Kid's friends call by. Welcome them in, insist they take a seat and have a cup of tea, and do not, under any circumstances, call upstairs to Emo Kid until the friend is comfortably settled in conversation with you. Emo Kid then has no choice but to join in. Feel free to ask questions like,

'So where did you get the money for those festival tickets?'

and actually get answers.

CONGRATULATIONS, SPECIAL AGENT EMO:

you have infiltrated the circle of trust.

EMO KID

In the Future

Unfortunately, Emo Kid's days are numbered. No, the Grim Reaper is not hovering above his head (though sometimes Emo Kid might wish it was).

At some point, Emo Kid is going to turn

30

and be forced to make some adult decisions, like getting a job.

Can you imagine Emo Kid slipping into a hot bubble bath to read the latest Jilly Cooper after a busy day at work? It could happen. And Emo Kid may have spent all day doing something like this…

ACCOUNTANT

Expert at telling the Inland Revenue his accounts are misunderstood. Frequently heard shouting, 'Why are you being so unfair?' down the phone at the end of every financial year.

TRAFFIC WARDEN

Often heard screaming, 'Why do you hate me?' at people who have just received a parking ticket, then smiling as he runs away.

TEACHER

Emo Teacher revisits the classroom nightmares that shaped him and is hellbent on taking the anti-emos into ever-lasting detention.

SURGEON

Behind that mask, who knows what Emo Surgeon is feeling? Patients who wake up mid-operation and see him hovering above with a scalpel in hand may suffer shock-induced heart attacks.

SOCIAL WORKER

Spending everyday in the company of seriously dysfunctional families makes his own teenage years seem relatively normal. No, no, they were hell.

BEAUTICIAN

All those years of practice with guyliner pay off at last. Tattoo territory beckons.

PSYCHIATRIST

Just for fun.

COULD I
Be Emo?

The whole emo thing isn't so scary now, is it! Feeling like all this research has changed something deep within you? Put you in touch with your emotional core?

Ultimately, it is all about being true to yourself. Stop pressuring yourself to be perfect – now it is time to focus on rebuilding your life from the ashes of your mistakes. Wear the clothes that really say something about who you are and what you are feeling at the moment.
Be true! Be emo!